FOR THE AFRICA YOGA PROJECT,

a program that educates, empowers, and employs youth from Africa using the practice of yoga. See their inspiring work at www.africayogaproject.org.

~ G.S.

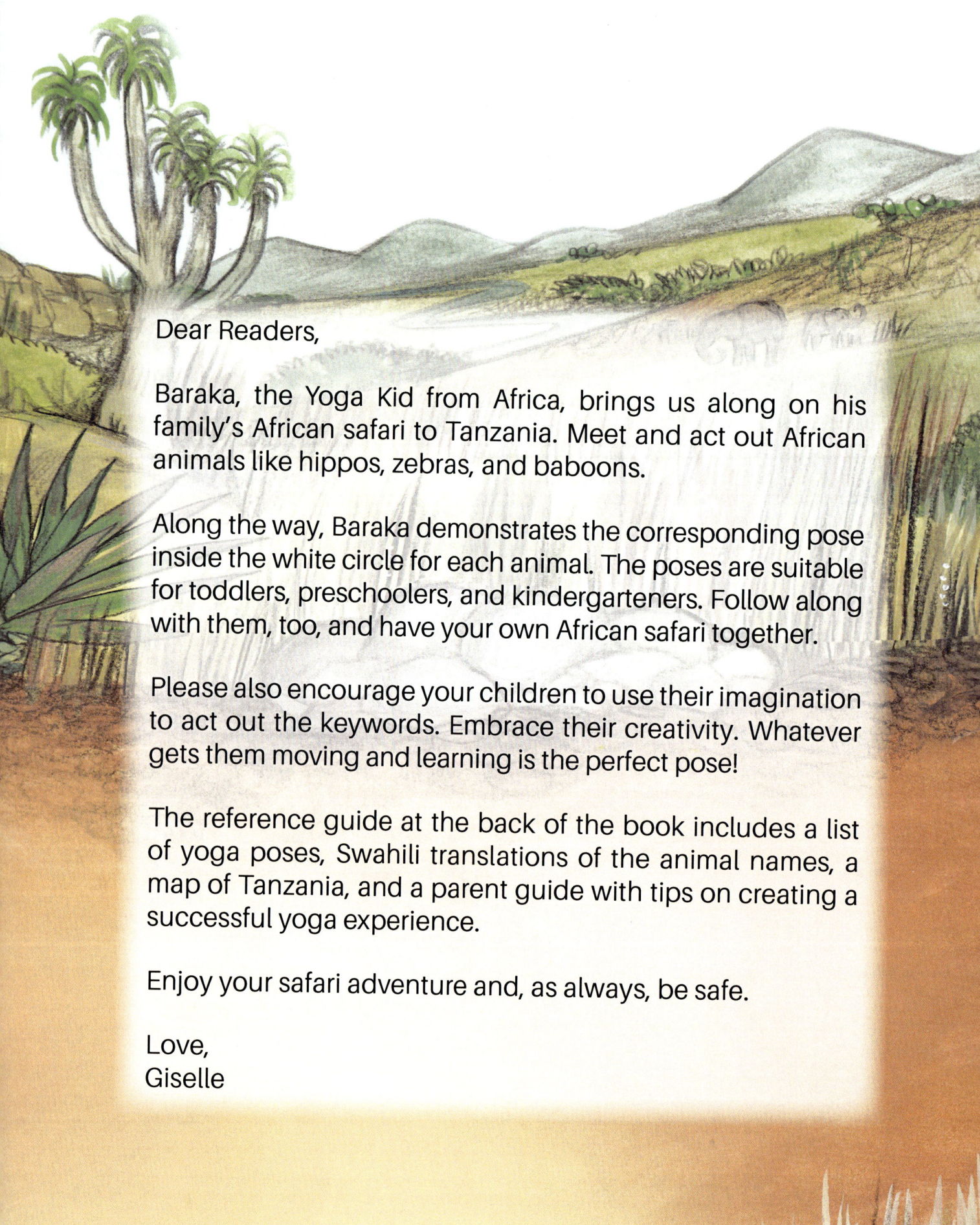

Dear Readers,

Baraka, the Yoga Kid from Africa, brings us along on his family's African safari to Tanzania. Meet and act out African animals like hippos, zebras, and baboons.

Along the way, Baraka demonstrates the corresponding pose inside the white circle for each animal. The poses are suitable for toddlers, preschoolers, and kindergarteners. Follow along with them, too, and have your own African safari together.

Please also encourage your children to use their imagination to act out the keywords. Embrace their creativity. Whatever gets them moving and learning is the perfect pose!

The reference guide at the back of the book includes a list of yoga poses, Swahili translations of the animal names, a map of Tanzania, and a parent guide with tips on creating a successful yoga experience.

Enjoy your safari adventure and, as always, be safe.

Love,
Giselle

123 AFRICAN SAFARI

A Kids Yoga Counting Book

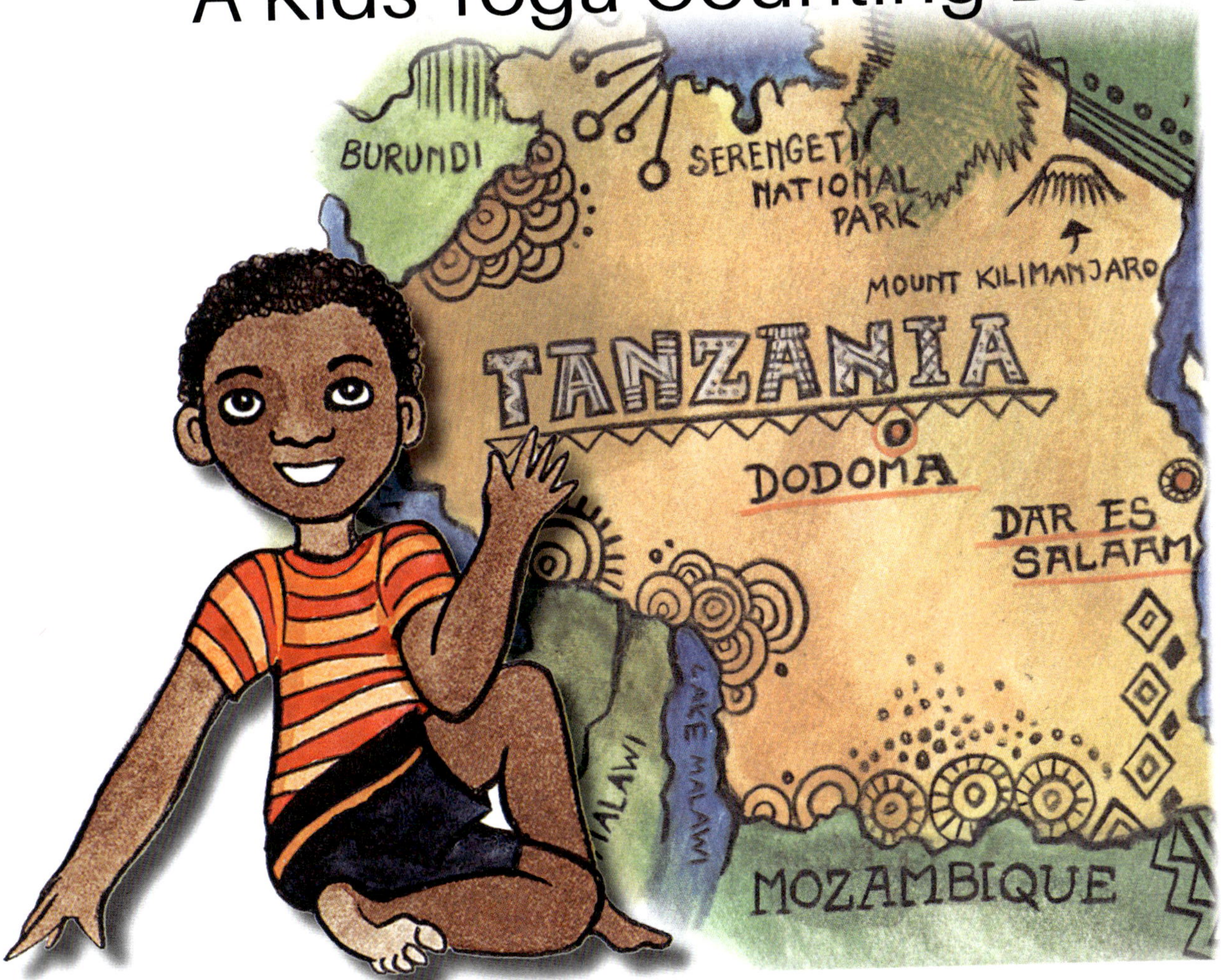

Written by Giselle Shardlow

Illustrated by Kirstin Eggers

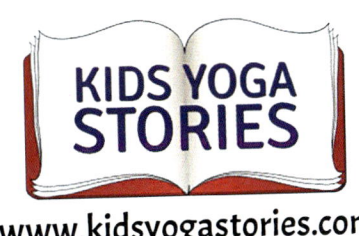

www.kidsyogastories.com

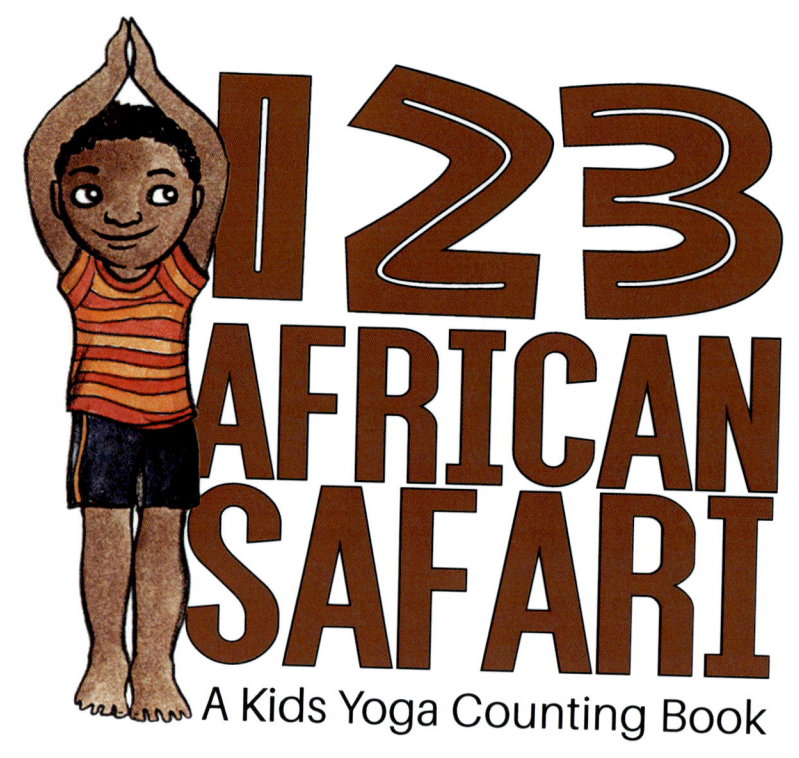

123 African Safari
A Kids Yoga Counting Book

Copyright © 2018 by Giselle Shardlow
Illustrations by Kirstin Eggers
All images © 2018 Giselle Shardlow

All rights reserved. No part of this book may be reproduced in any form by any electronic or mechanical means, including photocopying, recording, or information storage and retrieval without written permission from the author. The author, illustrator, and publisher accept no responsibility or liability for any injuries or losses that may result from practicing the yoga poses outlined in this storybook. Please ensure your own safety and the safety of the children.

ISBN-13: 978-1499719840

Kids Yoga Stories
Boston, MA
www.kidsyogastories.com
www.amazon.com/author/giselleshardlow
Email us at info@kidsyogastories.com
Ordering Information: Special discounts are available on quantity purchases by contacting the publisher at the email address above

What do you think? Let us know what you think of
123 African Safari at feedback@kidsyogastories.com.

Printed in the United States of America.

ONE GIRAFFE munches leaves from the branches of an acacia tree.

EXTENDED MOUNTAIN POSE

TWO WILDEBEESTS
snuggle together in the crater.

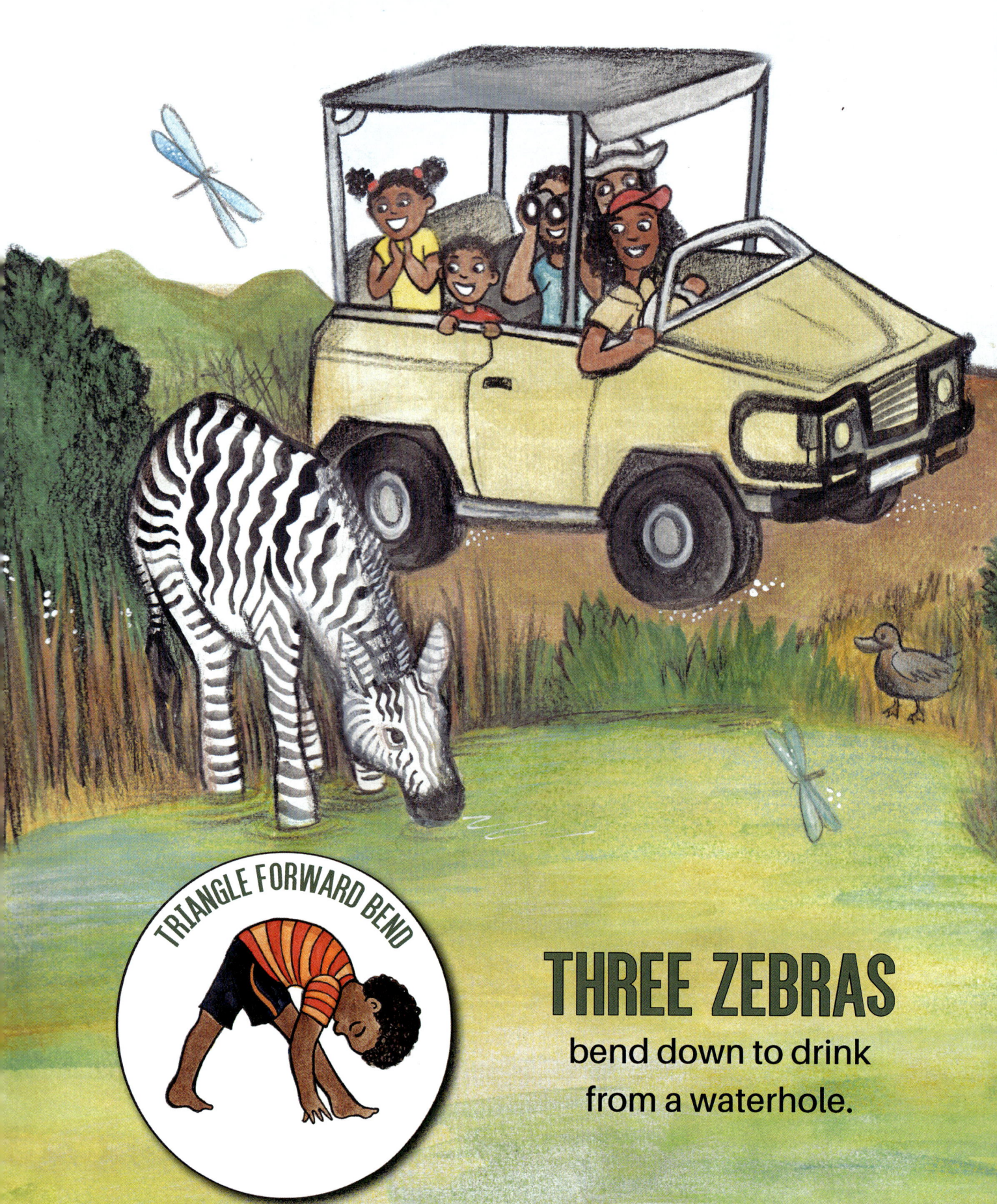

TRIANGLE FORWARD BEND

THREE ZEBRAS
bend down to drink from a waterhole.

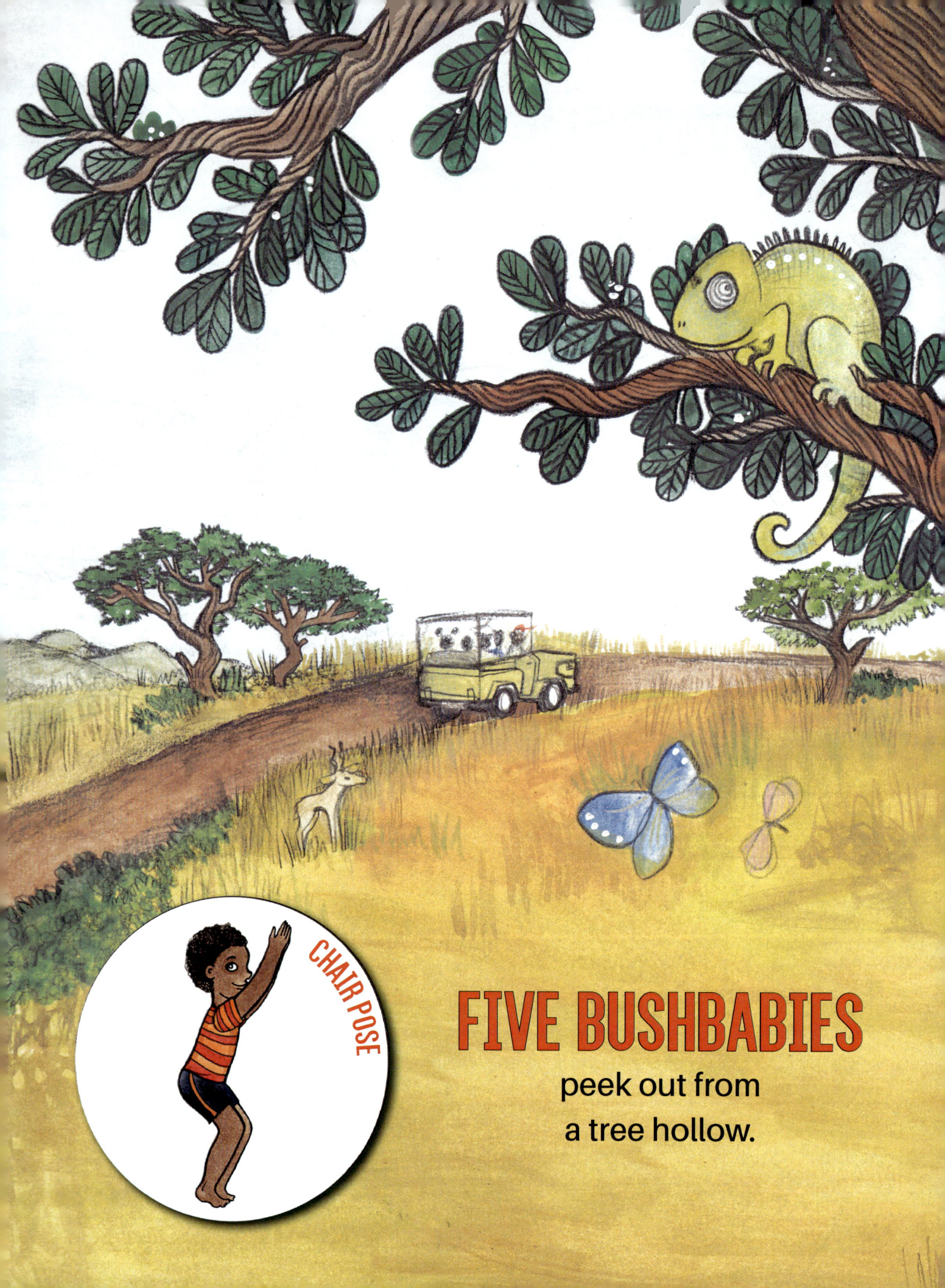

FIVE BUSHBABIES
peek out from a tree hollow.

CHAIR POSE

SIX ELEPHANTS
cool off in a refreshing mud bath.

SQUAT POSE

SEVEN BABOONS
sit on rocks in the woodlands.

EIGHT CHEETAHS
sprint across the arid plains.

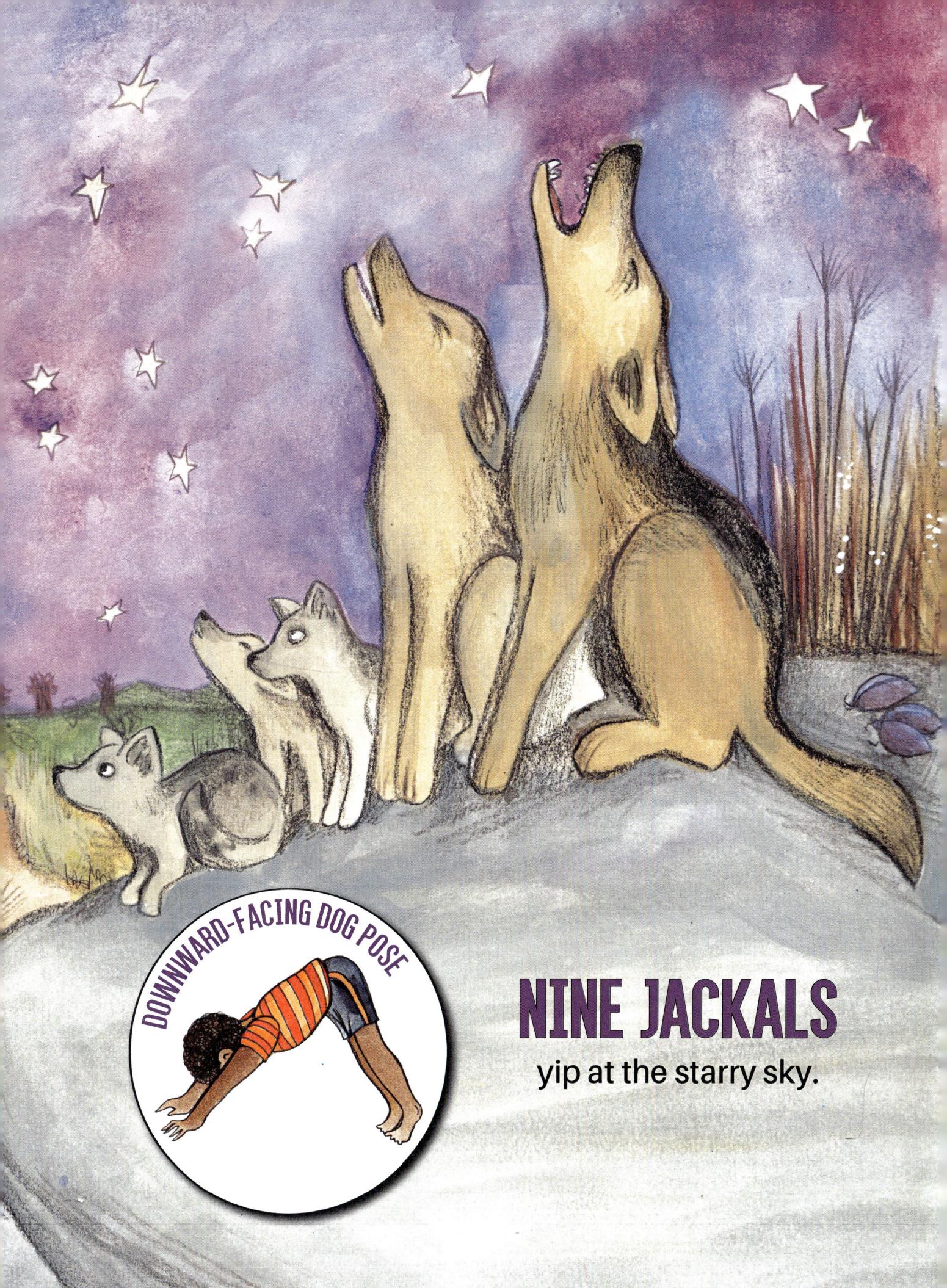

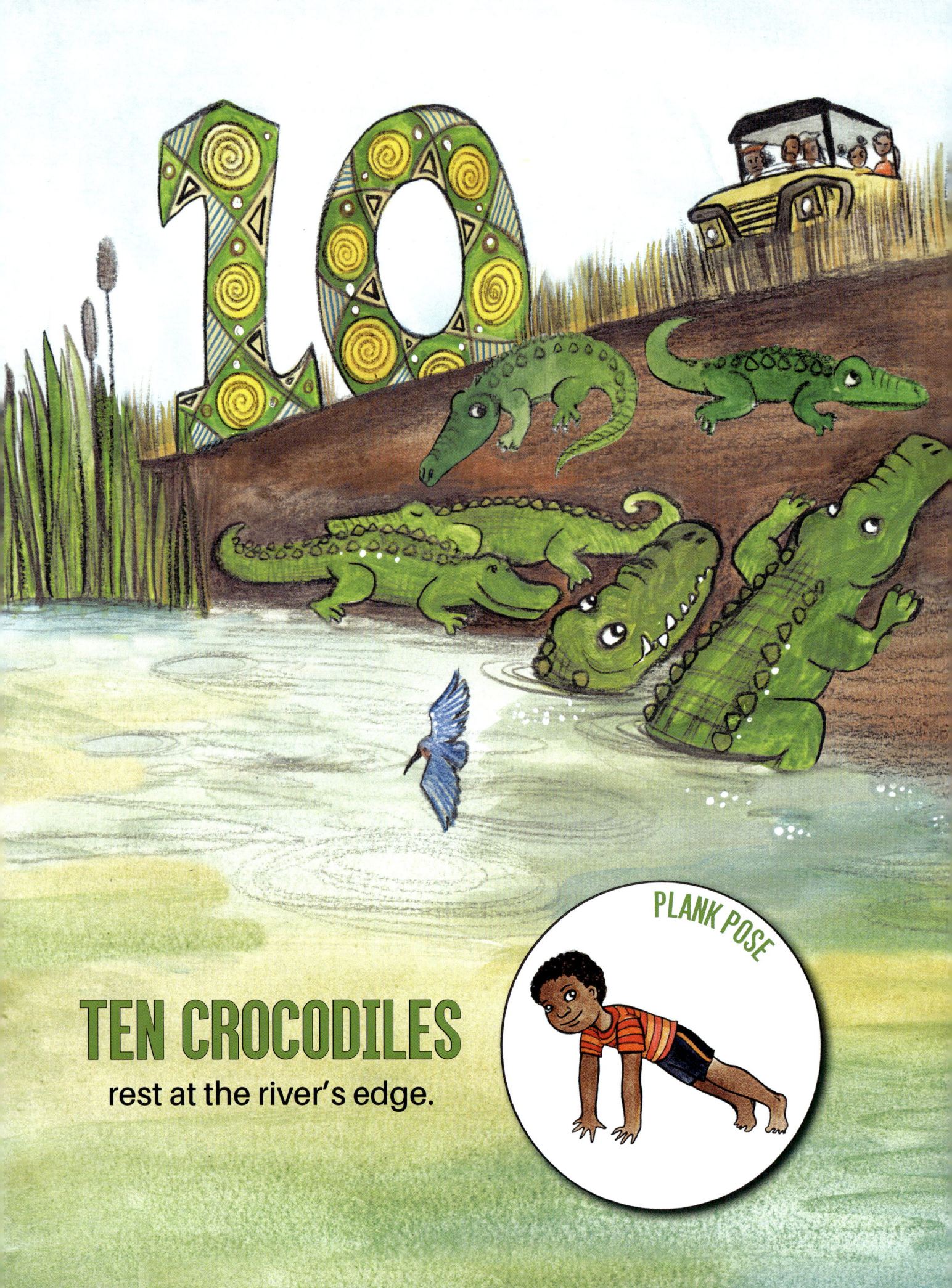

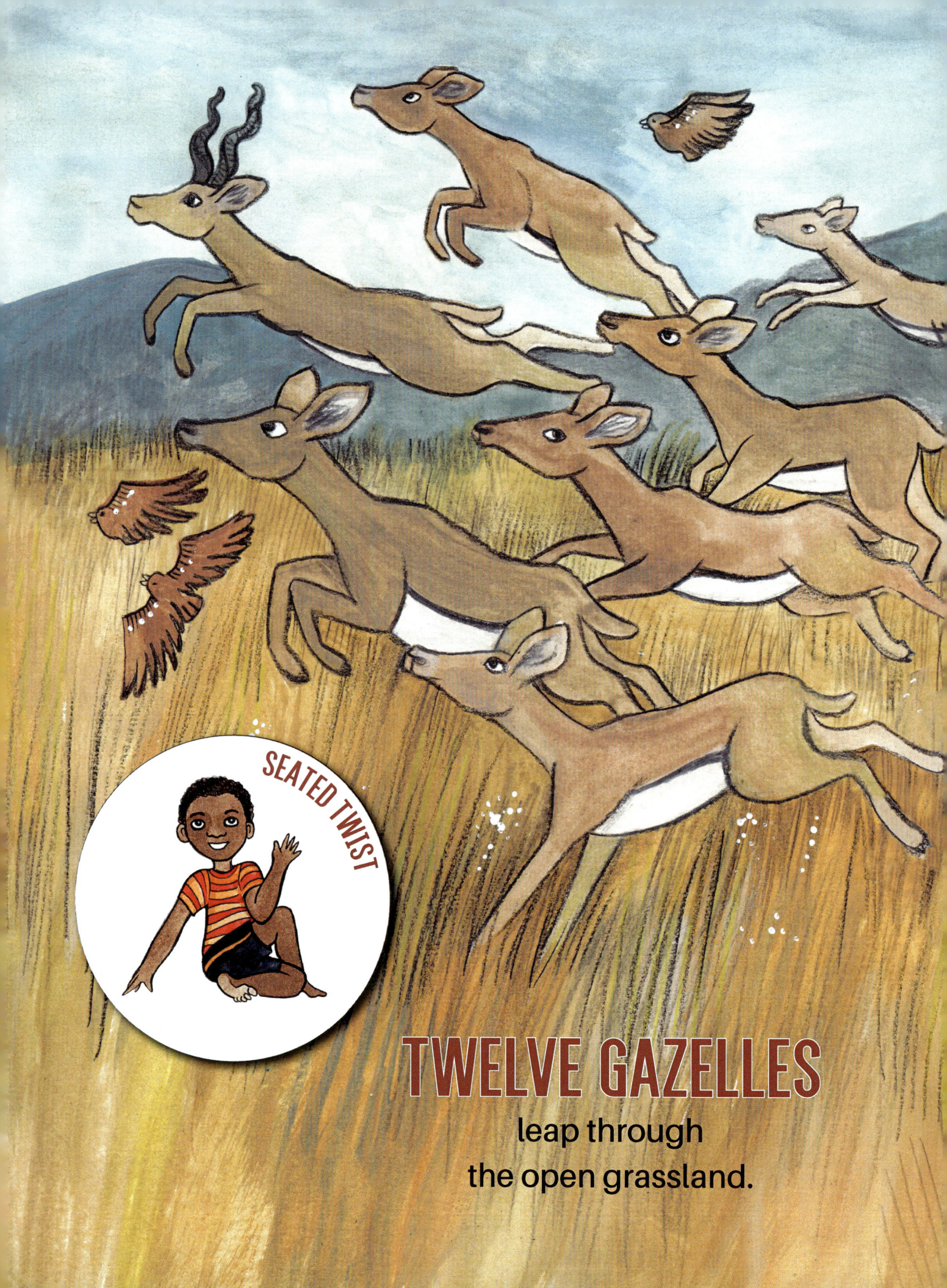

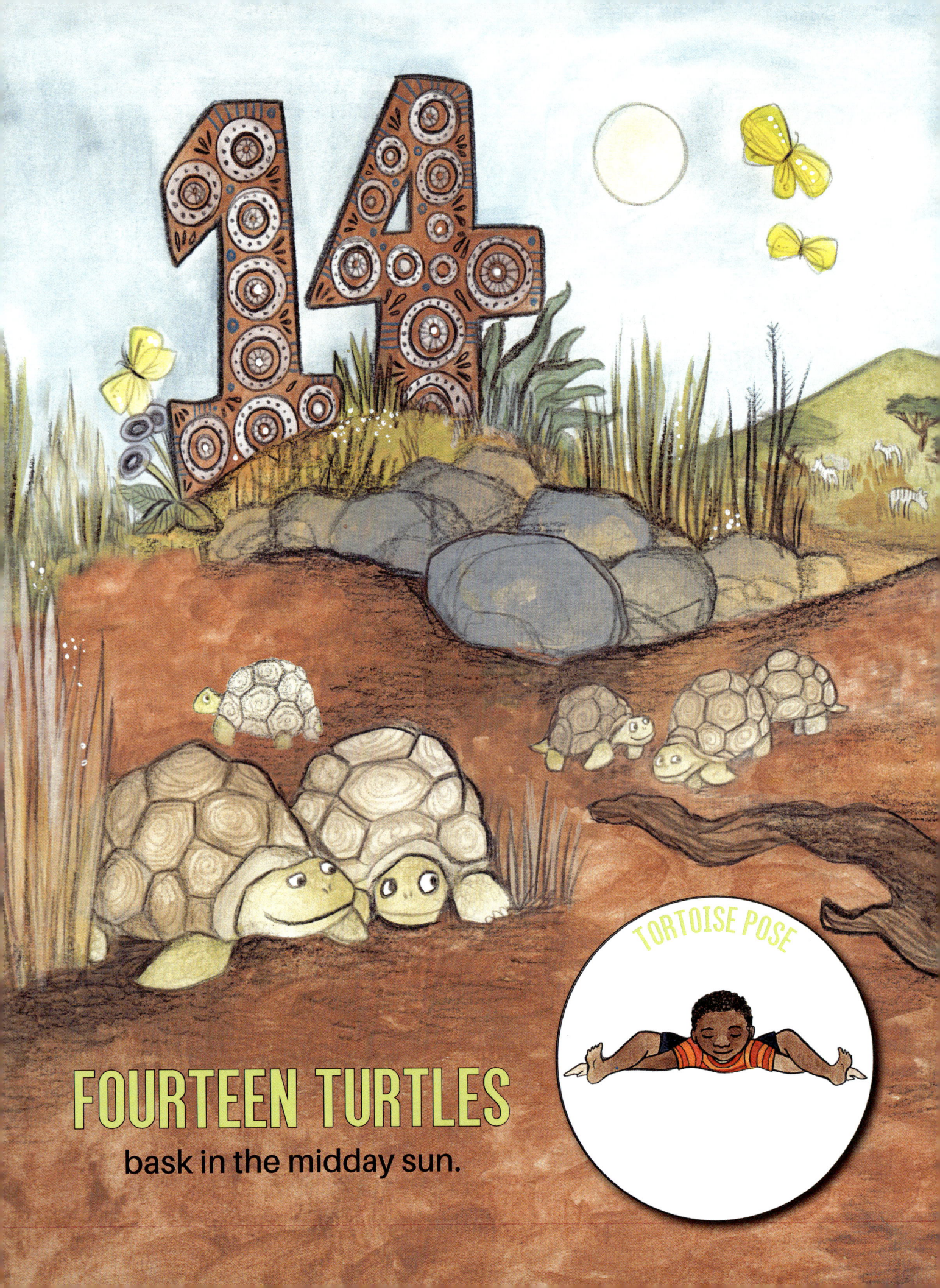

LIST OF KIDS YOGA POSES

The following list is intended as a guide only. Please encourage the children's creativity while ensuring their safety.

#	ANIMAL	YOGA POSE	DEMONSTRATION
1.	Giraffe	Extended Mountain Pose	
2.	Wildebeest	Warrior 1 Pose	
3.	Zebra	Triangle Forward Bend	
4.	Ostrich	Dancer's Pose	
5.	Bushbaby	Chair Pose	

#	ANIMAL	YOGA POSE
6.	Elephant	Wide-Legged Standing Forward Bend
7.	Baboon	Squat Pose
8.	Cheetah	Extended Cat Pose
9.	Jackal	Downward-Facing Dog Pose
10.	Crocodile	Plank Pose
11.	Hornbill	Pigeon Pose

#	ANIMAL	YOGA POSE	DEMONSTRATION
12.	Gazelle	Seated Twist	
13.	Hippo	Child's Pose	
14.	Turtle	Tortoise Pose	
15.	Lion	Resting Pose	

HOW TO PRACTICE THE YOGA POSES

The following list is intended as a guide only. Please encourage the children's creativity while ensuring their safety.

EXTENDED MOUNTAIN POSE: Stand tall in Mountain Pose, inhale, look up, and raise your arms straight up to the sky. Then exhale and bring your arms back down alongside your body. Repeat the inhale, raising and lowering your arms, for a few breaths. Pretend to be a giraffe reaching for the highest leaves.

WARRIOR 1 POSE: Step one foot back and bend your front knee. Reach both arms up over your head, pretending your arms are the curving horns of a wildebeest. Switch sides and repeat the steps.

TRIANGLE FORWARD BEND: Stand tall with legs hip-width apart, feet facing forward, and straighten your arms alongside your body. Take your right foot back, keeping your ankle bent at a thirty-degree angle. Place your hands on your hips, ensuring that your back is flat and that you are looking straight ahead. Then slowly bend forward as if your hips are a hinge, keeping a flat back and a long neck. Lastly, bring your hands to your shins, ankles, or the ground, depending on what feels comfortable, all the while checking that your spine is straight. Pretend to be a zebra bending down for a drink. Repeat on the other side.

DANCER'S POSE: Stand tall in Mountain Pose. Then stand on your right leg, reach your left leg out behind you, and place the outside of your left foot into your left hand. Bend your torso forward, with your right arm out in front for balance, and arch your leg up behind you. Pretend you're an ostrich cruising through the tall grasses. Switch sides and repeat the steps.

CHAIR POSE: Stand tall in Mountain Pose with your feet hip-width apart, bend your knees, and keep a straight spine. Hold your hands out in front of you. Pretend to be a bushbaby clinging to a tree.

 **WIDE-LEGGED FORWARD BEND:** Stand tall with legs hip-width apart, feet facing forward, and straighten your arms alongside your body. Step your feet out wide, bend your upper body, clasp your hands together, and pretend to be an elephant having a bath.

SQUAT POSE: Come down to a squat with your knees apart and your arms between your knees. Touch your hands to the ground. Pretend to be a baboon sitting on a rock.

 **EXTENDED CAT POSE:** Come to all fours, extend one leg out behind you, and look forward. Take the opposite arm out in front of you to counter balance. Pretend to be a cheetah sprinting across the plains. Repeat on the other side.

DOWNWARD-FACING DOG POSE: Step back to your hands and feet in an upside-down V shape, with your buttocks up in the air, and pretend to be a jackal stretching out on a rock.

 **PLANK POSE:** From Downward-Facing Dog Pose, come forward to balance on your palms and on your bent toes in a plank position. Keep your arms straight and your back long and flat. Pretend to be a crocodile resting on the riverbank.

PIGEON POSE: From an all-fours position, bring your right knee to rest behind your right hand, angling your right foot slightly inward. Gently take your buttocks down to the ground with your left leg extended straight out behind you. You might try placing a block under your right thigh. Keep your palms flat on the ground on either side of your right knee, look forward, keeping a straight spine. Pretend to be a hornbill perched on a branch. Repeat on the other side.

SEATED TWIST: Start by sitting cross-legged, bend your right knee, and place your right foot behind your left knee. Check that your spine is straight and your right foot is flat on the ground. Twist your upper body to the right. Take your left elbow to your right knee and your right hand back behind you. Pretend to be a graceful gazelle. Repeat on the other side.

CHILD'S POSE: Sit on your heels, slowly bring your forehead down to rest on the floor in front of your knees, rest your arms down alongside your body, and take a few deep breaths. Pretend to be a hippo wallowing in the river.

TORTOISE POSE: Sit on your buttocks with your knees bent and your feet flat on the floor. Then take your feet out wide and be sure you are sitting with a tall, straight spine. Slide your arms under your knees and place your hands flat on the floor outside your legs. Bend forward, keeping your back and neck straight. Pretend to be a turtle in its shell.

RESTING POSE: Lie on your back with your arms and legs stretched out. Breathe and rest. Pretend to be a lion in the shade.

COUNTING TO 15

1 Giraffe

2 Wildebeests

3 Zebras

4 Ostriches

5 Bushbabies

6 Elephants

7 Baboons

8 Cheetahs

9 Jackals

10 Crocodiles

11 Hornbills

12 Gazelles

13 Hippos

14 Turtles

15 Lions

AFRICAN CHEETAH: "DUMA"

BLACK-BACKED JACKAL: "MBWEHA"

NILE CROCODILE: "MAMBA"

RED-BILLED HORNBILL: "FILIMBI"

THOMSON'S GAZELLE: "PAA"

HIPPOPOTAMUS: "KIBOKO"

MARSH TERRAPIN: "KOBE"

AFRICAN LION: "SIMBA"

A SPECIAL THANK YOU

We would like to extend a special thank-you to Jody for verifying the behavior and group sizes of the African animals from her experience living on a reserve. Jody is a stay-at-home mom who is married to a career conservationist and is raising two girls in the Zambian bush. Before becoming a mother, Jody worked with international and environmental education. She is home-schooling her daughters, and she enjoys sharing her love of other cultures, nature, and conservation with them. She writes about their adventures at Mud Hut Mama (www.mudhutmama.com).

We would also like to thank Varya Sanina-Garmroud's husband and brother-in-law, who both verified the Swahili translations. Varya lives in China with her husband and two daughters. She is a philologist who is also trained as a Montessori educator, a perinatal fitness and Baby's First Massage Instructor, and a breastfeeding consultant. She blogs at Creative World of Varya (www.creativeworldofvarya.com) about parenting as well as nurturing and developing creativity, moral education, and multiculturalism.

MAP OF TANZANIA

KIDS YOGA STORIES GUIDE

This guide is intended for children's yoga teachers, primary school teachers, early childhood educators, parents, caregivers, homeschoolers, librarians, or grandparents—anyone who would like to experience the joy of yoga with young children.

PUT SAFETY FIRST. Ensure that the space is clear and clean. Spend some time clearing any dangerous objects or unnecessary items. A suitable space could be a classroom, school gymnasium, yoga studio, park, or your living room. Wear comfortable clothing and practice barefoot. Wait one to two hours after eating before practicing yoga.

PROPS ARE WELCOME. Lay out a yoga mat for each child, using the pattern that works for the space. Mats arranged in a circle seem to work best for younger age groups. Make sure that every child can see you. Towels could also be used as yoga mats on a non-slip surface. African-related props and music are a great addition.

CATER TO THE AGE GROUP. Use this Kids Yoga Stories book as a guide, but adapt according to the age of your children. Feel free to lengthen or shorten your journey to ensure that your children are fully engaged throughout your time together. Be aware of any physical or mental challenges that the children or a single child brings to the session and make appropriate revisions to the poses. Focus on the strengths of the children. My recommendation is to read the book with children ages two to six (toddlers to early primary). Break the journey down into a few poses for each session if you are working with ages two to four. Add more poses or extend the ideas if you're working with children over four years old. They might make up their own stories, invent their own poses, read books about Africa, take pictures of themselves in the poses, or paint pictures of the poses and keywords.

TALK TOGETHER. Engage your children in the book's topic. Talk about the keywords or traveling to different places so they can form meaningful connections. Explain the purpose, set expectations, and review the guidelines for the session. Be consistent and clear in your communication. This helps to set the tone, builds memory skills, and makes them feel safe and secure.

LEARN THROUGH MOVEMENT. Brain research shows that we learn best through physical activity. Our bodies are designed to be active. Encouraging your children to act out the keywords not only allows them to have fun, but also helps them learn about different places and techniques for active relaxation. Use repetition to engage the children and help them learn the movements. Ask your child to say or predict the next pose of the journey to Tanzania. Have them research Africa and find other people, places, or things that they can act out together.

LIGHTEN UP AND ENJOY YOURSELVES. A children's yoga experience is not as formal as an adult class. Encourage the children to use their creativity and provide them time to explore the postures. Avoid teaching perfectly aligned poses. The journey is intended to be joyful and fun. Your children feed off your passion and enthusiasm. Take the opportunity to energize yourself, as well. Read and act out the book together as a way to connect with each other. Whether it is two siblings or cousins, a grandparent and a grandchild, a teacher and a student, or a parent and a child, that connection is important. Bond with the little people in your life. Cherish the moment. Live in the present.

DEVELOP BREATH AWARENESS. Throughout the practice, feel free to bring attention to their inhale and exhale in a light-hearted way. For example, encourage the children to take a few deep breaths when they are in Child's Pose like a hippo. When you are in the final resting pose, do the Lion's Breath by opening your mouth, sticking out your tongue, and exhaling audibly.

RELAX. Allow your children time to end their session in Resting Pose for five to ten minutes. Massage their feet during or after their relaxation period. Relaxation techniques give children a way to deal with stress. Reinforce the benefits and importance of quiet time for their minds and bodies. Introduce meditation, which can be as simple as sitting quietly for a couple of minutes, as a way to bring stillness to their highly stimulated lives.

OOZE CREATIVITY, IMAGINATION, AND ABUNDANCE. Encourage each child to tap into his or her own creativity and imagination through movement and breath. Use the book as a springboard to other engaging learning activities. Welcome quiet times for reflection. Pause often. Remember, it's not at the end, but during the journey, where miracles happen.

ABOUT KIDS YOGA STORIES

We hope you enjoyed your Kids Yoga Stories experience.
Visit www.kidsyogastories.com to:

RECEIVE UPDATES.

For updates, contest giveaways, articles, and activity ideas,
sign up for our free Kids Yoga Stories Newsletter.

CONNECT WITH US.

Please share with us about your yoga journey. Send pictures of yourself practicing the poses or reading the story. Describe your journey on our social media pages (Facebook, Pinterest, Instagram, and Twitter).

CHECK OUT FREE STUFF.

Read our articles on books, yoga, parenting, and travel.
Download one of our kids yoga lesson plans or coloring pages.

READ OR WRITE A REVIEW.

Read what others have to say about our books or post your own review on Amazon or on our website. We would love to hear how you enjoyed this book.

Thank you for your support in spreading our message
of integrating learning, movement, and fun.

Giselle
Kids Yoga Stories
www.kidsyogastories.com
giselle@kidsyogastories.com
www.pinterest.com/kidsyogastories
www.facebook.com/kidsyogastories
www.twitter.com/kidsyogastories
www.amazon.com/author/giselleshardlow
www.goodreads.com/giselleshardlow

ABOUT THE AUTHOR

Giselle Shardlow draws from her experiences as a teacher, traveler, mother, and yogi to write her yoga stories for children. The purpose of her yoga books is to foster happy, healthy, and globally educated children. She lives in Boston with her husband and daughter.

ABOUT THE ILLUSTRATOR

Kirstin Eggers grew up in South Africa, Kenya, and France and completed her Illustration degree in Maidstone, England, in 2013. Since then, she has worked as a freelance illustrator on various children's books, magazines, album artwork, and anything else that came her way. Kirstin creates images in a variety of media from colored pencils to collage. She is inspired by mythology from around the world, historical and fantastical literature, and travel to faraway corners of the globe. For more of her work visit ww.kiki-kalahari.com.

OTHER YOGA BOOKS BY GISELLE SHARDLOW

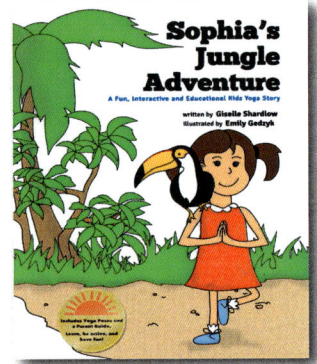
Sophia's Jungle Adventure

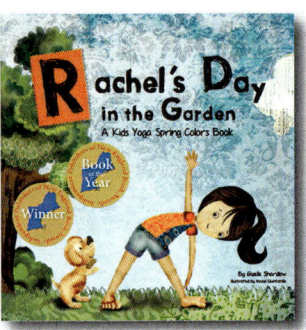
Rachel's Day in the Garden

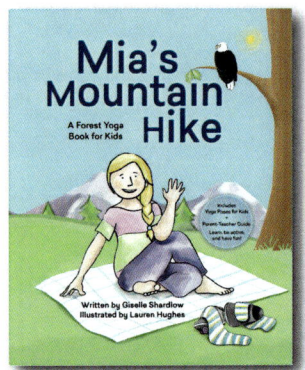
Mia's Mountain Hike

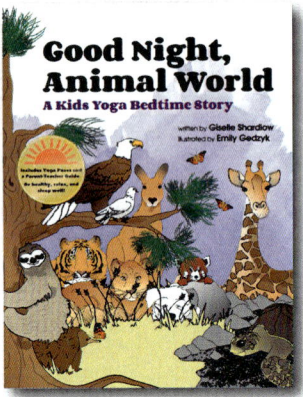
Good Night, Animal World

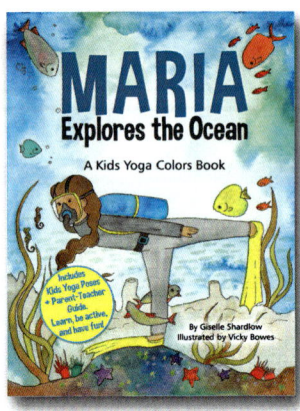
Maria Explores the Ocean

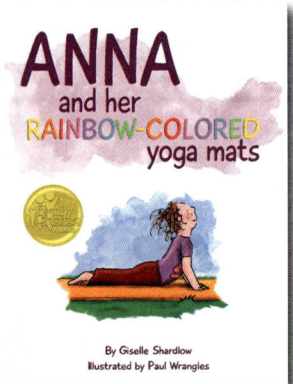
Anna and her Rainbow-Colored Yoga Mats

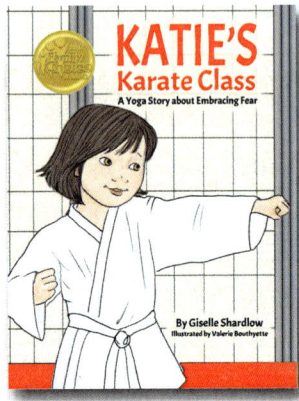
Katie's Karate Clas

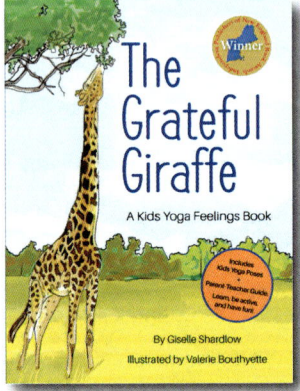
The Grateful Giraffe

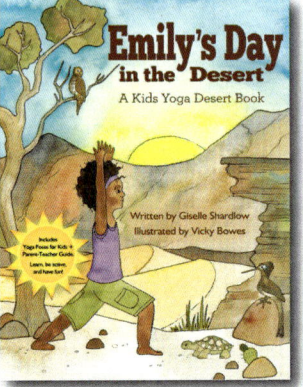
Emily's Day in the Desert

Many of the yoga books above are available in Spanish and eBook format.

www.kidsyogastories.com